Cursive Handwriting For Kids

with Aesop's Fables

Cursive Handwriting For Kids with Aesop's Fables

Translated by George Fyler Townsend

Edited by Michelle Morrow

Published by My Homeschool © 2023

ISBN: 978-0-6486045-0-1

Special thanks to "School Fonts" for use of their fonts and worksheet material.

To contact School Fonts their website is:

www.schoolfonts.com.au

This resource has been provided at a low cost to make it accessible to all. Copies of this can be made for students within one family. It is not transferable for sale. Apart from any fair dealing for the purposes of private study, research, criticism or review as permitted under the Copyright Act, no part may be reproduced for commercial use without the prior permission of the publisher.

All enquiries to My Homeschool

https://myhomeschool.com

Cover Design by Bethany Morrow.

ABOUT THIS BOOK

Unlock the timeless charm of cursive handwriting with Cursive Handwriting for Kids with Aesop's Fables.

Immerse your child in the world of beautiful penmanship as they journey through the enchanting tales of Aesop's Fables. This workbook offers a delightful blend of storytelling and skill-building, making the art of cursive writing an engaging adventure.

Our cursive handwriting copywork book improves vocabulary, strengthens literacy and encourages excellent handwriting.

Inside these pages, young learners will:

◊ Explore a collection of Aesop's beloved fables, igniting their imagination and moral understanding. With their guidance, your young learner will discover the art of crafting graceful, interconnected letters and words.

◊ Enhance their vocabulary while immersed n the wisdom of Aesop. Whether they're penning the timeless lessons of *The Tortoise and the Hare* or the cunning deeds of *The Fox and the Grapes*, each page becomes a delightful adventure through these cherished allegorical stories.

◊ Enrich their minds and nurture their creativity through stories and handwritten art, *Cursive Handwriting for Kids with Aesop's Fables* is the perfect tool to inspire a lifelong love for the written word. Watch as your child's handwriting flourishes, and their understanding of timeless virtues deepens, page by page.

Embark on a journey through the world of cursive handwriting and moral wisdom with this unique and captivating workbook. Ideal for children aged 7 and up, Cursive Handwriting for Kids with Aesop's Fables is an educational treasure that will leave a lasting impression on young hearts and minds.

TEACHING CURSIVE

In the days of inkwells and hard nibs children were taught to write a cursive script as their initial writing experience. From the age of six, children were expected to manage this handwriting script. Advocates for teaching cursive first believe that introducing cursive initially can:

◊ Provide more supervision when teaching cursive .

◊ Decrease 'B' and 'D' confusion.

◊ Help with special letter sequences lost with printing.

◊ Less writing fatigue because letters are joined in continuous strokes.

SKILLS THAT LEAD TO MASTERING WRITING.

Children learn to write by writing! Here are the stages that they progress through.

◊ Trace over letters.

◊ Print letters.

◊ Copy words.

◊ Copy sentences.

◊ Copy whole passages.

◊ Take dictation.

◊ Write narrations.

Ideally a child would not move on to the next step until the previous one is mastered.

COPYWORK

Practise handwriting with copywork—not composition! After a child has been taught a basic handwriting technique they need to improve their handwriting skills. How can they do that? The simple answer is with lots and lots of copywork.

Handwriting practice consists of *copying—not creating*! Remember that composition requires students to focus on content, organisation, spelling and punctuation. If handwriting perfection is also required, the frustration may be overwhelming, leading a child to avoid writing altogether.

During these formative years, the child will gradually become more adept at remembering what the letters look like and how they are formed; continued copywork reinforces this. After a time, a child will become more confident and begins introducing variations or deviations from the copybook form. This is the beginning of their own handwriting style.

Copywork is simply writing out by hand or copying from other written texts or models. This practice has been employed for centuries as a technique for teaching writing skills to young and old scholars. The primary use of copy work is for penmanship—to develop good technical skills. Practice makes perfect. Writing, however, is more than bending lines nicely and so copywork can also be of value in the following ways:

◊ as an aid for teaching correct spelling, a skill enhanced by seeing words and writing them correctly.

◊ exposing children to good literature and a variety of writing styles helps them recognise and use well-structured sentences, good grammar and correct punctuation.

◊ aids memorization,

◊ as a tried-and-tested method that works!

WHY IS COPYWORK SO GOOD?

Many handwriting books ask the child to copy a silly sentence while practising their writing technique. What a wasted opportunity! Copywork is much more than a handwriting program. Quality copywork uses fine literature, from great authors with excellent technique. Copy work has been used for centuries and is a recommended method for writing instruction by Charlotte Mason, Ruth Beechick, Laura Berquist and other classical educators.

> *'The earliest practice in writing proper for children of seven or eight should be, not letter writing or dictation, but transcription [copy work], slow and beautiful work...Transcription should be an introduction to spelling. Children should be encouraged to look at the word, see a picture of it with their eyes shut, and then write from memory....Double ruled lines, small text-hand, should be used at first, as children are eager to write very minute "small hand", and once they have fallen into this habit it is not easy to get good writing. A sense of beauty in their writing and in the lines they copy should carry them over this stage of their work with pleasure. Not more than ten minutes or a quarter of an hour should be given to the early writing lessons. If they are longer the children get tired and slovenly.'*

Charlotte Mason from Home Education

This book is the perfect companion for young learners, homeschoolers, and parents who want to make the art of handwriting a magical and memorable experience. Whether you're a fan of Beatrix Potter's timeless stories or simply looking to master the art of cursive, this book will whisk you away into a world of learning and imagination.

Join Aesop and his friends on a journey of letters, words, and wonder in *Cursive Handwriting for Kids with Aesop's Fables.* Let's get out the pencils and begin the adventure.

Aesop's Fables

The Cock and the Jewel

A cock, scratching for food for

himself and his hens, found a

precious stone and exclaimed: "If your

owner had found thee, and not I, he

would have taken thee up, and have

set thee in thy first estate; but I

have found thee for no purpose. I

would rather have one barleycorn than

all the jewels in the world.

The Traveller and His Dog

A traveller about to set out on a journey saw his dog stand at the door stretching himself. He asked him sharply: "Why do you stand there gaping? Everything is ready for you, so come with me instantly."

The dog, wagging his tail, replied:

"O, Master! I am quite ready; it is

you for whom I am waiting."

The loiterer often blames delay on his

more active friend.

The Mole and His Mother

A mole, a creature blind from birth,

once said to his mother: "I am sure

than I can see, Mother!" In the

desire to prove to him his mistake,

his mother placed before him a few

grains of frankincense, and asked,

"What is it?" the young mole said,

"It is a pebble."

His mother exclaimed: "My son, I am

afraid that you are not only blind, but

that you have lost your sense of smell.

The Swallow and the Crow

The swallow and the crow had

a contention about their plumage.

The crow put an end to the dispute

by saying, "Your feathers are

all very well in the spring, but mine

protect me against the winter."

Fair weather friends are not worth much.

The Mountain in Labour

A mountain was once greatly agitated.

Loud groans and noises were heard,

and crowds of people came from all

parts to see what was the matter.

While they were assembled in anxious

expectation of some terrible calamity, out

came a mouse.

Don't make much ado about nothing.

The Oxen and the Axle-Trees

A heavy wagon was being dragged

along a country lane by a team of oxen.

The axle-trees groaned and

creaked terribly; whereupon the oxen,

turning round, thus addressed the

wheels, "Hello there! Why do you make

so much noise? We bear all the

labour, and we, not you, ought to cry

out."

Those who suffer most cry out the

least.

The Boys and the Frogs

Some boys, playing near a pond, saw

a number of frogs in the water and

began to pelt them with stones. They

killed several of them, when one of

the frogs, lifting his head out of

the water, cried out:

"Pray stop, my boys: what is sport

to you, is death to us."

The Sick Stag

A sick stag lay down in a quiet

corner of its pasture ground. His

companions came in great numbers to

inquire after his health, and each one

helped himself to a share of the food

which had been placed for his use; so

that he died, not from his sickness,

but from the failure of the means of

living.

Evil companions bring more hurt than profit.

The Kid and the Wolf

A kid standing on the roof of a house, out of harm's way, saw a wolf passing by and immediately began

to taunt and revile him. The wolf,

looking up, said, "Sirrah! I hear

thee: yet it is not thou who mockest

me, but the roof on which thou art

standing."

Time and place often give the

advantage to the weak over the strong.

The Shepherd and the Wolf

A shepherd once found the whelp of

a wolf and brought it up, and after

a while taught it to steal lambs from

the neighbouring flocks. The wolf,

having shown himself an apt pupil

said to the shepherd, "Since you have

taught me to steal, you must keep a

sharp lookout, or you will lose some

of your own flock."

The Hawk, the Kite, and the Pigeons

The pigeons, terrified by the appearance of a kite, called upon the hawk to defend them. He at once consented. When they had admitted him into the cote, they found that he made more havoc and slew a

larger number of them in one day

than the kite could pounce upon in a

whole year.

Avoid a remedy that is worse than

the disease.

The Rivers and the Sea

The rivers joined together to complain

to the sea, saying, "Why is it that

when we flow into your tides so

potable and sweet, you work in us

such a change, and make us salty

and unfit to drink?"

The sea, perceiving that they intended

to throw the blame on him, said,

"Pray cease to flow into me, and then

you will not be made briny."

The Wild Boar and the Fox

A wild boar stood under a tree and

rubbed his tusks against the trunk.

A fox passing by asked him why he

thus sharpened his teeth when there

was no danger threatening from either

huntsman or hound. He replied, "I

do it advisedly; for it would never do

to have to sharpen my weapons just at

the time I ought to be using them."

The Flea and the Wrestler

A flea settled upon the bare foot of

a wrestler and bit him, causing the

man to call loudly upon Hercules for

help. When the flea a second time

hopped upon his foot, he groaned and

said, "O Hercules! if you will not

help me against a flea, how can I

hope for your assistance against greater

antagonists?'

The Farmer and the Fox

A farmer, who bore a grudge against

a fox for robbing his poultry yard,

caught him at last, and being determined

to take an ample revenge, tied some

rope well soaked in oil to his tail, and

set it on fire. The fox by a strange

fatality rushed to the fields of the

farmer who had captured him. It was

the time of the wheat harvest; but the

farmer reaped nothing that year and

returned home grieving sorely.

The Seagull and the Kite

A seagull having bolted down too large

a fish, burst its deep gullet-bag and lay

down on the shore to die. A kite

saw him and exclaimed: "You richly

deserve your fate; for a bird of the

air has no business to seek its food

from the sea."

Every man should be content to mind

his own business.

The Hare and the Hound

A hound started a Hare from his lair, but after a long run, gave up the chase. A goatherd seeing him stop, mocked him, saying "The little one is the best runner of the two."

The Hound replied, "You do not see

the difference between us: I was

only running for a dinner, but he

for his life."

The Bald Knight

A bald knight, who wore a wig,

went out to hunt. A sudden puff

of wind blew off his hat and wig, at

which a loud laugh rang forth from

his companions. He pulled up his

horse, and with great glee joined in

the joke by saying, "What a marvel it

is that hairs which are not mine

should fly from me, when they have

forsaken even the man on whose head

they grew."

The Lamp

A lamp, soaked with too much oil

and flaring brightly, boasted that it

gave more light than the sun. Then

a sudden puff of wind arose, and the

Lamp was immediately extinguished.

Its owner lit it again, and said:

"Boast no more, but henceforth be

content to give thy light in silence.

Know that not even the stars need to

be relit"

The Crab and the Fox

A crab, forsaking the seashore, chose

a neighboring green meadow as its

feeding ground. A fox came across

him, and being very hungry ate him

up. Seconds before being eaten, the

crab said, "I well deserve my fate,

for what business had I on the land,

when by my nature and habits I

am only adapted for the sea?'

Contentment with our lot is an element

of happiness.

The Woman and Her Hen

A woman possessed a hen that gave

her an egg every day. She often

pondered how she might obtain two

eggs daily instead of one, and at last, to

gain her purpose, determined to give the

Hen a double allowance of barley.

From that day the hen became fat and

sleek, and never once laid another egg.

The Boy Bathing

A boy bathing in a river was in

danger of being drowned. He called

out to a passing traveller for help, but

instead of holding out a helping hand,

the man stood by unconcernedly, and

scolded the boy for his imprudence. "Oh,

sir!" cried the youth, "pray help me

now and scold me afterwards."

Counsel without help is useless.

The Fox and the Grapes

A famished fox saw some clusters

of ripe black grapes hanging from a

trellised vine. She resorted to all her

tricks to get at them, but wearied herself

in vain, for she could not reach them.

At last she turned away, hiding her dis

appointment and saying, "The grapes are

sour, and not ripe as I thought."

The Wolf, the Fox, and the Ape

A wolf accused a fox stealing, but the

fox denied the charge. An ape undertook

to adjudge the matter between them.

When each had fully stated his case the

ape announced said, "I do not think

you, Wolf, ever lost what you claim;

and I do believe you, Fox, to have

stolen what you so stoutly deny."

The dishonest, if they act honestly, get

no credit.

The Lion and the Three Bulls

Three bulls for a long time pastured

together. A lion lay in ambush in

the hope eating them, but was afraid

to attack them while they kept together.

Having at last by guileful speeches

succeeded in separating them, he attacked

them without fear as they fed alone,

and feasted on them one by one at

his own leisure.

Union is strength.

The Gnat and the Bull

A gnat settled on the horn of a

bull, and sat there a long time.

Just as he was about to fly off, he

made a buzzing noise, and inquired of

the bull if he would like him to go.

The bull replied, "I did not know

you had come, and I shall not miss

you when you go away."

Some men are of more consequence in

their own eyes than in the eyes of

their neighbours.

The Dog and the Oyster

A dog, used to eating eggs, saw an

oyster and, opening his mouth to its

widest extent, swallowed it down with

the utmost relish, supposing it to be

an egg. Soon afterwards suffering

great pain in his stomach, he said, "I

deserve all this torment, for my folly

in thinking that everything round must

be an egg."

They who act without sufficient thought,

will often fall into unsuspected danger.

The Wolf in Sheep's Clothing

A wolf resolved to disguise in sheep

skin to secure food more easily. He

pastured with the flock deceiving the

shepherd by his costume. In the

evening the shepherds shut the fox in

the fold. During the night the

shepherds came to the fold to obtain

meat for the next day, and mistakenly

caught up the wolf instead of a

sheep, and killed him instantly.

Harm seek. harm find.

The Dogs and the Hides

Some dogs famished with hunger saw

a number of cowhides steeping in a

river. Not being able to reach them,

they agreed to drink up the river,

but it happened that they burst

themselves with drinking long before

they reached the hides.

Attempt not impossibilities.

The Hare and the Tortoise

A hare one day ridiculed the short

feet and slow pace of the tortoise, who

replied, laughing: "Though you be swift

as the wind, I will beat you in a race."

The hare, believing her assertion to be

simply impossible, assented to the

proposal; and they agreed that the fox

should choose the course and fix the

goal. On the day appointed for the race

the two started together. The Tortoise

never for a moment stopped, but went

on with a slow but steady pace straight

to the end of the course.

The hare, lying down by the wayside,

fell fast asleep. At last waking up,

and moving as fast as he could, he

saw the tortoise had reached the goal,

and was comfortably dozing after her

fatigue.

Slow but steady wins the race.

The Mischievous Dog

A dog used to run up quietly to the heels of everyone he met, and to bite them without notice. His master put a bell about his neck so that others would know he was coming.

Thinking it a mark of distinction, the

dog grew proud of his bell and went

tinkling it all over the marketplace.

One day an old hound said to him:

"Why do you make such an exhibition

of yourself? That bell that you carry

is not, believe me, any order of merit,

but on the contrary a mark of disgrace,

a public notice to all men to avoid

you as an ill mannered dog."

Notoriety is often mistaken for fame.

The Shepherd's Boy and the Wolf

A shepherd boy, who watched a flock

of sheep near a village, brought out

the villagers three or four times by

crying out, "Wolf! Wolf!" and when

his neighbours came to help him,

laughed at them for their pains. The

wolf, however, did truly come at last.

The shepherd boy, now really alarmed,

shouted in an agony of terror:

"Pray, do come and help me; the wolf

is killing the sheep;" but no one paid

any heed to his cries, nor rendered

any assistance. The wolf, having no

cause of fear, at his leisure lacerated

or destroyed the whole flock.

There is no believing a liar, even

when he speaks the truth.

The Mice in Council

The mice summoned a council to decide

how they might best devise means of

warning themselves of the approach of

their great enemy the cat.

Among the many plans suggested, the

one that found most favour was the

proposal to tie a bell to the neck of

the cat, so that the mice, being warned

by the sound of the tinkling, might

run away and hide themselves in their

holes at his approach. But when the

mice further debated who among them

should thus "bell the cat," there was

no one found to do it.

The Hunter and the Woodman

A timid hunter, was in search of lion

tracks. He asked a woodsman if he

had seen the lions footprints or knew

where his lair was. "I will show you

the lion." said the woodsman.

The hunter, looking scared said, "No,

I did not ask that; it is his track

only I am in search of, not the lion

himself."

The hero is brave in deeds as well

as words.

The Hen and the Golden Eggs

A cottager and his wife had a hen

that laid a golden egg every day.

They supposed that the hen must

contain a great lump of gold inside.

To get the gold they killed it. Having

done so, they found to their surprise

that the hen differed in no respect

from their other hens. The foolish

pair, hoping to become rich at once,

deprived themselves of the gain of

which they were assured day by day.

The Peacock and the Crane

A peacock spreading its gorgeous

tail mocked a crane that passed by,

ridiculing the ashen hue of its

plumage and saying, "I am robed,

like a king, in gold and purple and

all the colours of the rainbow; while

you have not a bit of colour on your

wings."

"True," replied the crane; "but I soar

to the heights of heaven and lift up

my voice to the stars, while you walk

below, like a cock, among the birds

of the dunghill."

Fine feathers don't make fine birds.

The Town Mouse and the Country Mouse

A country mouse invited a town

mouse, an intimate friend, to pay him

a visit and partake of his country

fare.

As they were on the bare ploughlands,

eating there wheat stocks and roots

pulled up from the hedgerow, the

town mouse said to his friend, "You

live here the life of the ants, while

in my house is the horn of plenty. I

am surrounded by every luxury, and

if you will come with me, as I wish

you would, you shall have an ample

share of my dainties."

The country mouse was easily

persuaded, and returned to town with

his friend. On his arrival, the town

mouse placed before him bread,

barley, beans, dried figs, honey,

raisins, and, last of all, brought a

dainty piece of cheese from a basket.

The country mouse, being much

delighted at the sight of such good

cheer, expressed his satisfaction in

warm terms and lamented his own

hard fate. Just as they were beginning

to eat, someone opened the door, and

they both ran off squeaking, as fast

as they could, to a hole so narrow

that two could only find room in it

by squeezing. They had scarcely begun

their repast again when someone else

entered to take something out of a

cupboard, whereupon the two mice,

more frightened than before, ran away

and hid themselves. At last the country

mouse, almost famished, said to his

friend: "Although you have prepared

For me so dainty a feast, I must

leave you to enjoy it by yourself. It

is surrounded by too many dangers to

please me. I prefer my bare ploughlands

and roots from the hedgerow, where I

can live in safety, and without fear."

The Crow and the Pitcher

A CROW perishing with thirst saw a

pitcher, and hoping to find water, flew to

it with delight. When he reached it, he

discovered to his grief that it contained

so little water that he could not possibly

get at it. He tried everything he could

think of to reach the water, but all his

efforts were in vain. At last he collected

as many stones as he could carry and

dropped them one by one with his beak

into the pitcher, until he brought the water

within his reach and thus saved his life.

Necessity is the mother of invention.

The Flies and the Honey-Pot

A NUMBER of Flies were attracted to a jar of honey which had been overturned in a housekeeper's room, and placing their feet in it, ate greedily. Their feet, however, became so smeared with the honey that they

could not use their wings, nor release

themselves, and were suffocated. Just as

they were expiring, they exclaimed, "O

foolish creatures that we are, for the sake

of a little pleasure we have destroyed

ourselves."

Pleasure bought with pains, hurts.

The Astronomer

AN ASTRONOMER used to go out at night to observe the stars. One evening, as he wandered through the suburbs with his whole attention fixed on the sky, he fell

accidentally into a deep well. While he

lamented and bewailed his sores and

bruises, and cried loudly for help, a

neighbour ran to the well, and learning

what had happened said: "Hark ye, old

fellow, why, in striving to pry into what

is in heaven, do you not manage to see

what is on earth?"

The North Wind and the Sun

THE NORTH WIND and the Sun

disputed as to which was the most

powerful, and agreed that he should be

declared the victor who could first strip a

wayfaring man of his clothes. The North

Wind first tried his power and blew with

all his might, but the keener his blasts,

the closer the Traveller wrapped his cloak

around him, until at last, resigning all

hope of victory, the Wind called upon the

Sun to see what he could do. The Sun

suddenly shone out with all his warmth.

The Traveller no sooner felt his genial rays

than he took off one garment after another,

and at last, fairly overcome with heat, un

dressed and bathed in a stream that lay in

his path.

Persuasion is better than Force.

The Dogs and the Hides

SOME DOGS famished with hunger saw a

number of cowhides sleeping in a river.

Not being able to reach them, they agreed

to drink up the river, but it happened that

they burst themselves with drinking long

before they reached the hides.

Attempt not impossibilities.

The Old Woman and the Wine Jar

AN OLD WOMAN found an empty jar which had lately been full of prime old wine and which still retained the fragrant smell of its former contents. She greedily placed it several times to her nose, and drawing it backwards and forwards said,

"O most delicious! How nice must the

Wine itself have been, when it leaves

behind in the very vessel which contained it

so sweet a perfume!"

The memory of a good deed lives.

www.ingramcontent.com/pod-product-compliance
Lightning Source LLC
Chambersburg PA
CBHW061807290426
44109CB00031B/2961